LOOKING FOR THE LOST SHEEP

STORIES JESUS TOLD

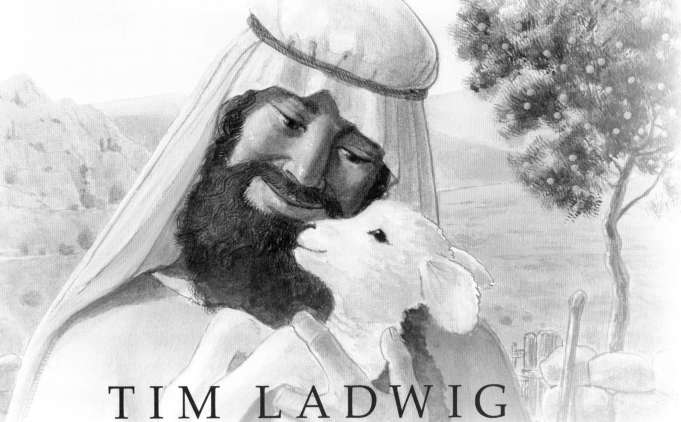

TIM LADWIG

Award-Winning Illustrator of Psalm Twenty-Three

Our Daily Bread
Publishing™

For Briana, Makayla, and David

–TL

Looking for the Lost Sheep

Illustrations © 2020 by Tim Ladwig

Parent letter © 2020 by Our Daily Bread Publishing

ISBN: 978-1-62707-967-9

Printed in China

20 21 22 23 24 25 26 27 / 8 7 6 5 4 3 2 1

Now the tax collectors and sinners were all gathering around to hear Jesus.

But the Pharisees and the teachers of the law muttered, "This man welcomes sinners and eats with them."

Then Jesus told them this parable:

Suppose one of you has a hundred sheep

and loses one of them.

Doesn't he leave the ninety-nine
in the open country

and go after the lost sheep

until he finds it?

And when he finds it,

he joyfully puts it on his shoulders

and goes home.

Then he calls his friends and neighbors together and says, "Rejoice with me; I have found my lost sheep."

I tell you that in the same way there will be more rejoicing in heaven over one sinner who repents than over ninety-nine righteous persons who do not need to repent.

Dear Parent,

We hope you find this book as exciting to read to your kids as it was for Tim to illustrate. Jesus's words, spoken 2,000 years ago, can still teach our children—and us!

We can all identify with losing something important to us. Of course, Jesus used an illustration from His day—when everyone knew a lot more about sheep. Today, we may think of our panic when we lost our car keys or the family pet got away. Remember the joy when someone yelled, "I found it!"?

Far too many people—kids included—are wandering around lost in our society. Our children need to know that there is One who is always seeking us—always desiring to come to our rescue. And His name is Jesus.

As you read this story with your children, maybe you can guide their understanding of Jesus's parable of the lost sheep with these questions:

- A parable is a story that teaches an important lesson. Why do you think Jesus chose to tell a story about sheep to show what it means to find something that was missing?

- When we look at other parts of the Bible (like John 10), we understand that the person in the story looking for the lost sheep is meant to be Jesus, or God. Why is He looking for just one sheep when He has so many other sheep?

- Imagine if you were lost, and Jesus was looking everywhere for you. Imagine Him finding you, and then picking you up and carrying you on His shoulders to take you home. How would you feel?

- Can you imagine what it means that there is "rejoicing in heaven"? Who is in heaven to rejoice?

—From the Our Daily Bread for Kids team